Get set... GO!

Vegetables

Judy Bastyra

Photography by Michael Michaels

Contents

Watts Books

London • New York • Sydney

About vegetables

Some vegetables can be eaten either raw or cooked:

cabbage

onions

peppers

carrots

Other vegetables have to be cooked before you can eat them:

leeks

sweetcorn

potatoes

broccoli

cauliflower

Some vegetables can be scrubbed or peeled...

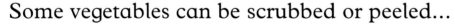

turnips

potatoes

onion

...but some can be eaten just as they are:

cucumber   tomatoes   celery   radishes

All vegetables should be washed before you eat them.
Always cut vegetables on a board using a sharp knife.

HOW TO USE A VEGETABLE PEELER

✔ Hold the peeler by the handle.

✔ Place it against the skin of
the vegetable.

✔ Scrape downwards.

✔ Always work downwards,
never upwards.

✔ Turn the vegetable as you peel.

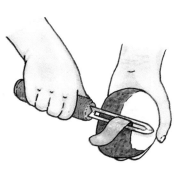

10 golden cooking rules

✔ Wash your hands 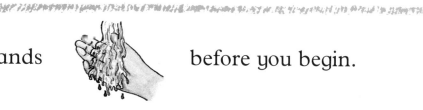 before you begin.

 ✔ Read the whole recipe carefully.

✔ Make sure you have all the ingredients
and equipment you need.

✔ Measure out the ingredients carefully.

✔ Allow at least 15 minutes time
for the oven to warm up.

✔ Wear an apron

to protect your clothes.

✔ Use a separate spoon
if you want to taste the mixture.

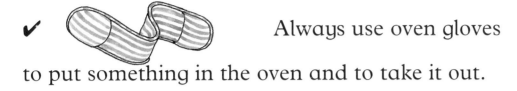 Always use oven gloves

to put something in the oven and to take it out.

✔ Always turn the handle of

a saucepan on the stove to one side.

✔ Finally, don't forget to do the washing up!

GUIDE TO THE MEASUREMENTS USED
tbl/tbls – *tablespoon/s*   tsp/tsps – *teaspoon/s*
g – *grams*   ml – *millilitres*

 Wherever you see this symbol,
it means that you should
ask for help from an adult.

Sticks and dip

Get ready

- ✔ 175g frozen spinach, defrosted
- ✔ Vegetables, such as carrots, cucumber and baby corn
- ✔ Small pot sour cream
- ✔ 2 tbls mayonnaise
- ✔ Salt and pepper
- ✔ Paper kitchen towels
- ✔ Knife and peeler

...Get set

Defrost the spinach in a bowl.
Drain in a sieve and pat dry
with paper kitchen towels.
Peel and trim the vegetables.
Cut them into sticks or slices.

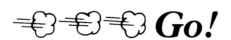 Go!

Mix the spinach with the sour cream.
Add the mayonnaise and salt and pepper.
Serve the dip with the vegetables.

Oven chips

Get ready

✔ 2 potatoes ✔ Peeler ✔ Biscuit cutters

✔ 2 carrots ✔ Saucepan ✔ Roasting tin

✔ 60ml oil ✔ Colander

✔ Knife

✔ SET THE OVEN TO 230°C/450°F/GAS MARK 8

...Get set

Peel the carrots and cut into sticks.

Peel the potatoes and cut into thick slices.

Boil the potatoes for about 5 minutes, then drain and leave to cool.

Cut into shapes with the biscuit cutters.

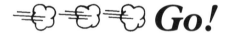 **Go!**

Put the vegetable chips and oil in the roasting tin.

Bake for half an hour, turning once.

Mashed potato forest

Get ready

- ✔ 2 potatoes
- ✔ 1 tbl butter
- ✔ 1 tbl milk
- ✔ Salt
- ✔ 8 broccoli florets
- ✔ 4 mushrooms, sliced
- ✔ 75g grated cheese
- ✔ Yellow pepper
- ✔ Peeler and knife
- ✔ Saucepan
- ✔ Potato masher
- ✔ Heatproof plate
- ✔ SET THE GRILL TO MEDIUM

...Get set

Peel the potatoes and cut into cubes.
Boil in salted water for 10 minutes.
Mash in butter, milk and half the cheese.
Boil the mushrooms and broccoli until tender.
Cut a sun shape from the pepper.

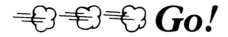 **Go!**

Spread the potato over the plate.
Make a picture on top with the other vegetables.
Top with remaining cheese and grill for 5 minutes

Carrot muffins

Get ready

✔ 300g plain flour ✔ 150g brown sugar ✔ Bowl

✔ Half a tsp salt ✔ 2 eggs ✔ Spoon

✔ 2 tsps baking powder ✔ 180ml milk ✔ Paper ca

✔ 2 tsps cinnamon ✔ 150g melted butter   cases

✔ 2 tbls sultanas ✔ 2 carrots, grated

✔ SET THE OVEN TO 200°C/400°F/GAS MARK 6

...Get set

Mix the dry ingredients together.
Beat the eggs, butter and milk together.
Stir the dry mixture into the wet mixture.
Add the grated carrots and sultanas.

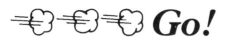 Go!

Spoon the mixture into the paper cases.
Bake in the oven for 20–25 minutes.

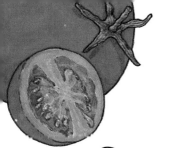

Tomato owls

Get ready

- ✔ Different sized tomatoes
- ✔ Small tin tuna
- ✔ 2 tbls mayonnaise
- ✔ Hard-boiled egg
- ✔ Stuffed green olives
- ✔ 2 tsps tomato sauce
- ✔ Knife
- ✔ Mixing bowl
- ✔ Fork and spoon

...Get set

Halve the tomatoes and scoop out the seeds.
Mash the tuna and egg with the fork.
Mix in the mayonnaise and tomato sauce.

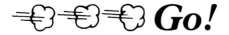 **Go!**

Pile some tuna mixture into one tomato half.
Cut the other one into triangles
to make a beak and ears for decoration.
Add an olive cut in half as eyes.

Sweetcorn bake

Get ready

- ✔ 1 chopped onion
- ✔ 2 tbls oil
- ✔ 300g can sweetcorn
- ✔ 1 egg, beaten
- ✔ 25g grated Cheddar cheese
- ✔ Frying pan
- ✔ Ovenproof dish
- ✔ Wooden spoon
- ✔ SET THE OVEN TO 180°C/350°F/GAS MARK 4

...Get set

Heat the oil in the frying pan.
Add the onion and cook for 5 minutes.
Put the onion in the dish
along with the sweetcorn and cheese.
Stir in the egg.

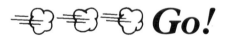 **Go!**

Bake in the centre of the oven
for 45 minutes until firm.
Serve immediately.

16

Sweet pepper kebabs

Get ready

✔ Yellow, green, orange
　 and red sweet peppers

✔ 2 tbls tomato sauce

✔ Half a tsp Worcestershire sauce

✔ 2 tbls water

✔ SET THE GRILL TO MEDIUM

✔ Knife and spoon

✔ Heart-shaped
　 biscuit cutters

✔ Kebab skewers

✔ Basting brush

...Get set

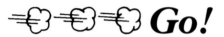

Cut the peppers in quarters and remove the seeds.
Cut heart shapes with the biscuit cutter.
Thread them on to the skewers.
Mix the other ingredients together for the sauce.

Go!

Put the kebabs on the grill pan.
Brush the sauce over the peppers.
Grill for 10 minutes, turning once.

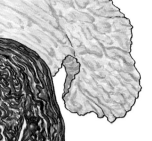

Christmas tree salad

Get ready

✔ Lettuce, washed
✔ Red cabbage
✔ Cucumber
✔ Celery stick

✔ Sweet peppers
✔ Half a tsp mustard
✔ 2 tbls cider vinegar
✔ 6 tbls olive oil

✔ Knife
✔ Large plate
✔ Jam jar and l

...Get set

Slice the lettuce and cabbage finely.
Arrange them in a triangle on the plate.
Add a celery trunk and a bucket
cut from pepper at the bottom.
Cut other pepper shapes to decorate.

 **Go!**

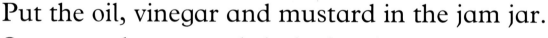

Put the oil, vinegar and mustard in the jam jar.
Screw on the top and shake hard.
Pour the dressing over the salad and serve.

20

Cucumbermobile

Get ready

- ✔ Cucumber
- ✔ 75g cream cheese
- ✔ 2 radishes
- ✔ Hard-boiled egg
- ✔ Knife
- ✔ Toothpicks

...Get set

Cut the cucumber in half crossways.
Scoop out the seeds from one half.
Fill it with cream cheese.
Put half the egg on top to make the driver's body.
Fix a radish on top with a toothpick as his head.

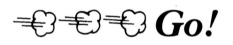 **Go!**

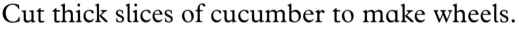

Cut thick slices of cucumber to make wheels.
Make cucumber arms, a hat
and a steering wheel for the driver.
Slice a radish in half for headlights.
Stick on using toothpicks.

Index

First published in 1994 by
Watts Books
96 Leonard Street
London EC2A 4RH

Franklin Watts Australia
14 Mars Road
Lane Cove
NSW 2066

Editor: Pippa Pollard
Design: Ruth Levy
Cover design: Shoba Mucha
Artwork: Ruth Levy

Special thanks to Charles
Bradley, assistant food designer
and stylist.
Thanks also to Aroma for
crockery used p.7

A CIP catalogue record for this
book is available from the
British Library

Dewey Decimal Classification:
641.6

UK ISBN 0 7496 1496 X

10 9 8 7 6 5 4 3 2 1

© 1994 Watts Books

Printed in Malaysia